THE Flying Girl

How Aída de Acosta Learned to Soar

Margarita Engle

Illustrated by Sara Palacios

atheneum

ATHENEUM BOOKS FOR YOUNG READERS
New York   London   Toronto   Sydney   New Delhi

I THANK GOD FOR THE COURAGE OF WOMEN PIONEERS IN EVERY FIELD.

For information, I'm grateful to the Smithsonian Institution, the New Jersey State Library, and the International Women's Air & Space Museum.

For encouragement, I'm thankful to Curtis and the rest of our family, and to Angelica Carpenter, Sandra Ríos Balderrama, and Joan Schoettler.

For hard work and dedication, I'm grateful to my wonderful agent, Michelle Humphrey; my editor, Reka Simonsen; the illustrator, Sara Palacios; and the entire publishing team.

—M. E.

Many thanks to the International Women's Air & Space Museum for providing reference materials.

—S. P.

ATHENEUM BOOKS FOR YOUNG READERS
An imprint of Simon & Schuster Children's Publishing Division
1230 Avenue of the Americas, New York, New York 10020
Text copyright © 2018 by Margarita Engle
Illustrations copyright © 2018 by Sara Palacios
All rights reserved, including the right of reproduction in whole or
in part in any form.
ATHENEUM BOOKS FOR YOUNG READERS is a registered trademark of
Simon & Schuster, Inc. Atheneum logo is a trademark of Simon & Schuster, Inc.
For information about special discounts for bulk purchases,
please contact Simon & Schuster Special Sales at 1-866-506-1949 or
business@simonandschuster.com.
The Simon & Schuster Speakers Bureau can bring authors to your live event.
For more information or to book an event, contact the Simon & Schuster Speakers Bureau
at 1-866-248-3049 or visit our website at www.simonspeakers.com.
The text for this book was set in Goudy Oldstyle.
The illustrations for this book were rendered in mixed media: gouache, markers,
colored pencil, pencil, and digital.
Manufactured in China
1217 SCP
First Edition
10 9 8 7 6 5 4 3 2 1
Library of Congress Cataloging-in-Publication Data
Names: Engle, Margarita, author. | Palacios, Sara, illustrator.
Title: The flying girl : how Aída de Acosta learned to soar / Margarita Engle ;
illustrated by Sara Palacios.
Description: First edition. | New York : Atheneum Books for Young Readers, [2017] |
Audience: Ages 4-8. | Audience: K to grade 3. | Includes bibliographical references.
Identifiers: LCCN 2015045504 | ISBN 9781481445023 (hardcover : alk. paper) |
ISBN 9781481445030 (eBook)
Subjects: LCSH: Acosta, Aida de, 1884–1962—Juvenile literature. | Santos-Dumont,
Alberto, 1873–1932—Juvenile literature. | Women air pilots—United States—Biography—
Juvenile literature. | Women in aeronautics—History—Juvenile literature. | Airships—
Juvenile literature.
Classification: LCC TL540.A38 E54 2017 | DDC 629.13092—dc23
LC record available at http://lccn.loc.gov/2015045504

For my daughter, Nicole, with love
—M. E.

To Mom, Dad, and my husband, Ed, for helping me fly
—S. P.

One day, a girl named Aída was strolling
on a lively street in a lovely city
when she glanced up and was dazzled
by the sight of a huge balloon
that glided as gracefully
as a whale-shaped moon.

Below the balloon, an air boat dangled,
and inside, there was a man.

"If that man can fly, so can I," cried Aída.
"All I need are some lessons
and a chance to try!"

Aída's mother scolded, "No, no, no,
silly girl, don't be so bold. Ay, *ay*, *ay*,
no one will ever marry a girl
who dares to fly!"

But Aída had a dream now,
a wild dream of soaring,
and she did not care to marry
anyone who thought dreams
were boring.

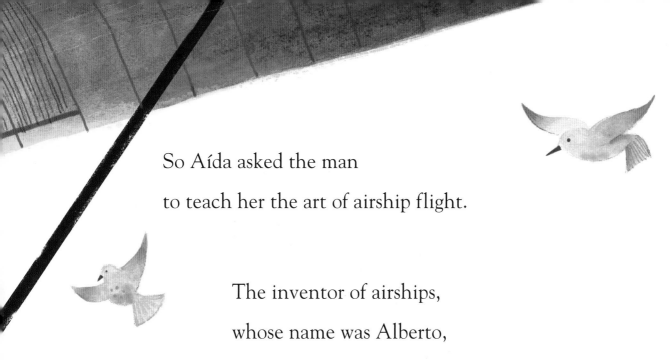

So Aída asked the man
to teach her the art of airship flight.

The inventor of airships,
whose name was Alberto,
agreed to show Aída
how to start a motor and steer,
turn left, turn right . . .

Lessons on the ground weren't easy,
but Aída worked hard and soon learned
how to pull this lever, tug that rope,
drop more ballast,
believe,
practice,
hope!

One evening Alberto invited Aída
to an aerial dinner with tables as tall
as elephants, served by waiters
who walked on tilted stilts
that
made
them
look
like
silly
giraffes.

At dinner Alberto said that his airships
were meant to be chariots of peace,
so that people all over the world
could meet one another
and develop friendships
by flying back and forth.

When Alberto invited Aída to ride while he
drove an airship, she cried, "No, no, no!
Ay, *ay*, *ay*, I won't be a passenger.
I only want to be
the pilot!"

Alberto was amazed.
Aída was just a teenager,
and no woman or girl had ever flown before.
But no one had believed
Alberto's wild dream of motorized flight
could come true either.
Not until he invented his airship.

So Alberto realized that if he could fly,
Aída could too. All she needed
was courage and a chance
to try.

On a clear summer day,
Aída finally had her thrilling chance
to pull this lever, tug that rope,
drop more ballast,
believe,
rise up,
hope!

Like a whale-shaped moon,

the airship's enormous balloon

soared above the busy city and

out to the countryside.

It sailed over green farms,

and cows and sheep,

high above the heads

of excited children

who cried out, "Look, look—

it's a girl, and she's flying!"

From her dangling air boat, Aída smiled down at the children, but then she frowned at Alberto, who was on a road far below, frantically pedaling his bicycle and waving a handkerchief, as he tried to show her which way to go—even though she had already told him that she did not need help because she had practiced.

Alberto got tangled in a thicket
of trees and fell far behind.

Aída kept flying high above roads and rivers,

completely alone,

truly free . . .

until finally, she reached

her destination: a green field

where swift polo ponies

twirled and leaped

like dancers.

Aída landed skillfully,

planning to watch the daring game,

but down on the ground, she soon found

that she could not climb out

of the air boat.

Her dress was too fancy.

The skirt was too tight.

So she wriggled

while children giggled

until, in the end, some helpful men

had to tip the boat sideways

so that she could slide out,

almost gracefully,

without too much

of a bumpy,

toppling

tumble.

Aída tried to watch the horses,
but angry strangers surrounded her,
shouting, scolding, calling names,
saying she was too bold, too brave,
too different, too strange.

Girls, they hollered, should only be allowed

to learn how to cook, sew, and clean,

but girls, they bellowed, should never

be taught how to fly

huge machines.

Just then, Alberto finally caught up,
still pedaling his bicycle, eager to cheer her.

"You did it!" he shouted. "You flew! You're a hero,
such a brave inspiration for all the girls
of the world!"

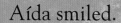

Aída smiled.

Aída laughed.

Yes, yes, yes! Ay, *ay*, *ay*, she really was the first,

but she was sure she would not be

the last.

Every child who had seen her

glide so high above roads and fields

was probably already singing:

"If that young lady can fly, so can I,

all I need are some lessons

and a chance

to try!"

"Sometimes," Aída said to Alberto,
"all it takes to change the whole world
is one wild dreamer's
soaring example."

Aída de Acosta

(1884–1962) is known as the first woman of powered flight. She was born in New Jersey to a Cuban father and Spanish mother. At the age of nineteen, during a trip to Paris, Aída became fascinated by the airships of Brazilian inventor Alberto Santos-Dumont. She took three lessons on the ground, at his private airpark in Neuilly St. James, where Alberto built the dirigibles that he referred to as "chariots of peace." After Aída attended one of Alberto's quirky "aerial dinners"—with seven-foot-high tables, and waiters on stilts—he invited her to ride in an airship. She insisted that she wanted to be the pilot, not a passenger.

Aída's mother disapproved, but she agreed to let her daughter fly on the condition that the flight be kept secret from Aída's father, because in those days, girls who made news were not considered respectable.

Aída's historic flight to the Château de Bagatelle polo field near Paris took place in the summer of 1903, nearly six months before the Wright Brothers flew a fixed-wing airplane. When a spectacular photo of Aída's flight appeared in newspapers, her father discovered her secret and demanded that she never speak of her accomplishment. Aída was an obedient daughter, so she kept her promise until the 1930s, when she donated her papers to the Smithsonian, where they were displayed along with the engine of the airship she had flown.

As the wife of Charles Lindbergh's lawyer, Aída retained a lifelong interest in aviation, but after losing an eye to glaucoma, she directed her courage toward eye care advocacy. She raised funds for the first eye institute in the United States, at Johns Hopkins Hospital, and directed the first eye bank in America, the Eye-Bank for Sight Restoration, Inc., in New York.

Alberto Santos-Dumont is known in his native Brazil as the father of aviation. Inspired by Jules Verne novels, he began inventing flying machines at the age of ten, on the remote coffee plantation where he grew up. His dirigible flights around the Eiffel Tower in Paris were some of the great spectacles of early aviation. Unlike the Wright Brothers, Alberto did not believe in patents, and when he won prizes, he donated most of the money to the poor. He became a leader of the protest movement against military use of aviation technology.